THE MAGNIFICENT BOOK OF CREATURES OF THE ABYSS

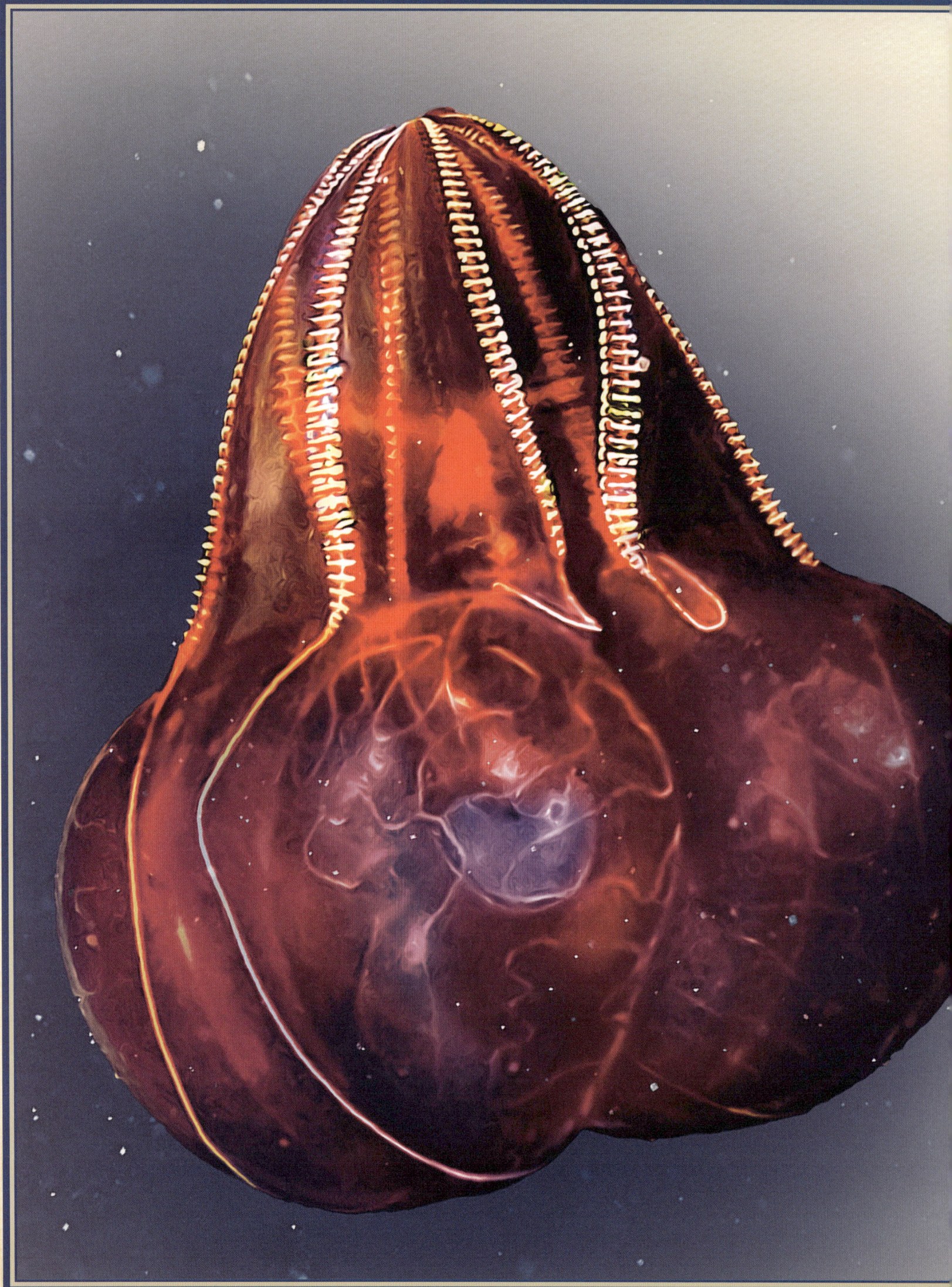

THE MAGNIFICENT BOOK OF CREATURES OF THE ABYSS

ILLUSTRATED BY
Val Walerczuk

WRITTEN BY
Bethanie and Josh Hestermann

weldon**owen**

Written by Bethanie and Josh Hestermann
Illustrated by Val Walerczuk
Additional illustrations by Isabel Aracama and Simon Mendez

weldon**owen**

Copyright © 2023 Weldon Owen Children's Books

All rights reserved. No part of this publication may be reproduced, distributed, or transmitted in any form or by any means, including photocopying, recording, or other electronic or mechanical methods, without the prior written permission of the publisher, except in the case of brief quotations embodied in critical reviews and certain other noncommercial uses permitted by copyright law.

Weldon Owen would like to thank the Monterey Bay Aquarium Research Institute and the National Oceanic and Atmospheric Administration for their permission to use their photographs as art references. We would also like to thank the Woods Hole Oceanographic Institution for its permission to use photos for the pink see-through fantasia, black swallower and gulper eel as art references. Gulper eel photo by Paul Caiger © Woods Hole Oceanographic Institution. We are grateful to Dr. Alexander Ziegler and Dr. Chong Chen for their permission to use their photos of the emperor dumbo octopus and scaly-foot snail respectively as art references. Humpback anglerfish: Doug Perrine / Alamy Stock Photo

Weldon Owen Children's Books
An imprint of Weldon Owen International, L.P.
A subsidiary of Insight International, L.P.
PO Box 3088
San Rafael, CA 94912
www.insighteditions.com

Weldon Owen Children's Books:
Designed by Claire Cater
Edited by George Maudsley
Assistant Editor: Pandita Geary
Senior Production Manager: Greg Steffen
Art Director: Stuart Smith
Publisher: Sue Grabham

Insight Editions:
Publisher: Raoul Goff

ISBN: 9781915588289
Manufactured, printed, and assembled in China
First printing, TOP1022
23 22 21 20 19 1 2 3 4 5

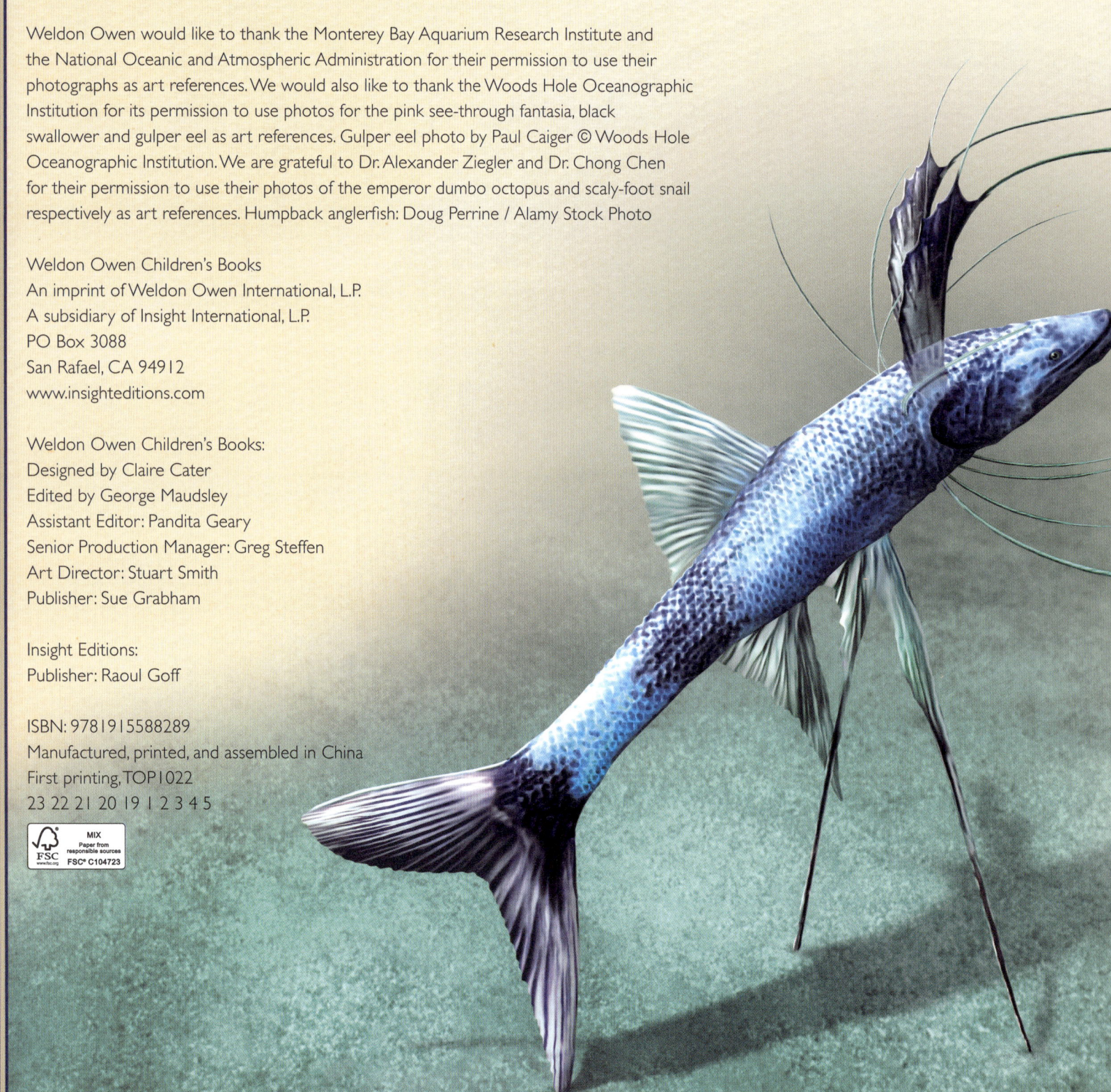

Introduction

There are places in the ocean that no human has ever seen. If you could sink down to the cold, dark abyss, you would find a world unlike any other – a dangerous world under crushing pressure, where underwater volcanoes spit toxic chemicals and there is hardly anything to eat.

Descend about 200 metres (660 feet) into the ocean, and you will catch the last glimpses of sunlight filtering down from the surface. Drop below 1,000 metres (3,300 feet) and the eerie glow of strange creatures becomes the only thing lighting the depths. Here, in the deepest ocean layers, fanged predators lurk in the inky blackness that extends for miles and miles. Even in one of the harshest places on Earth, there is life.

The Magnificent Book of Creatures of the Abyss takes you on an underwater journey to the deepest parts of the ocean. Encounter worms that eat bones, a snail with an iron shell and a sponge with a glass skeleton. Meet a fish that has a see-through head, a squid with one huge eye and one small one, and a comb jelly that shimmers like a rainbow. Discover what kind of creature drops glowing green bombs on its enemies and which fish lives deeper than any other.

Uncover some of the ocean's most fascinating secrets on your voyage through the depths. In the abyss, you never know what is hiding in the dark.

Fact file

Lives: Worldwide, except the poles

Depth: 900–4,700 m (2,950–15,400 ft)

Length: Up to 43 cm (1 ft 5 in)

Diet: Zooplankton

Discovered: 1886

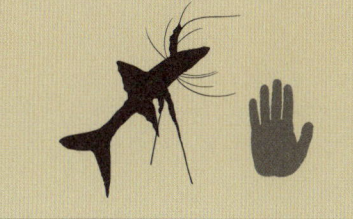

Contents

Pink see-through fantasia	8
Vampire squid	10
E.T. sponge	12
Deep-sea siphonophore	14
Scaly-foot snail	16
Shining bomber worm	18
Deep-sea brittle star	20
Blob sculpin	22
Gulper eel	24
Humpback anglerfish	26
Giant tubeworm	28
Goblin shark	30
Sparks' two-armed ctenophore	32
Black swallower	34
Giant isopod	36
Bigfin squid	38
Tripod fish	40

Barreleye	42	Bloodybelly comb jelly	60
Giant deep-sea nudibranch	44	Mariana snailfish	62
Common fangtooth	46	Dandelion siphonophore	64
Emperor dumbo octopus	48	Strawberry squid	66
Whalefish	50	Greenland shark	68
Zombie worm	52	Giant phantom jelly	70
Sea pig	54	Pom-pom anemone	72
Owlfish	56	Pacific viperfish	74
Sperm whale	58	Balloon worm	76
		Piglet squid	78

Pink see-through fantasia

Enypniastes eximia

- The pink see-through fantasia is a type of sea cucumber. But unlike most sea cucumbers, this one swims. It swims through the deep ocean on a constant search for its next meal.

- The fantasia is also known as the headless chicken monster because it looks like a chicken without a head. A sea cucumber does not really have a head, just a mouth surrounded by tentacle-like tube feet.

- After landing on the sea floor, the pink see-through fantasia uses its tube feet to shovel whatever it can find to eat into its mouth. It then swims off to continue its journey.

- This fantasia is well named because its pink skin is completely see-through. All its internal organs are visible – even the food inside a fantasia's intestine can be seen after it has eaten!

- Pink see-through fantasias are not always pink. They can also be a reddish-brown or purple and tend to get darker as they grow.

- When in danger, a pink see-through fantasia lights up, and its skin will stick to anything that tries to attack it. The glowing skin clings to and distracts the predator while the fantasia gets away.

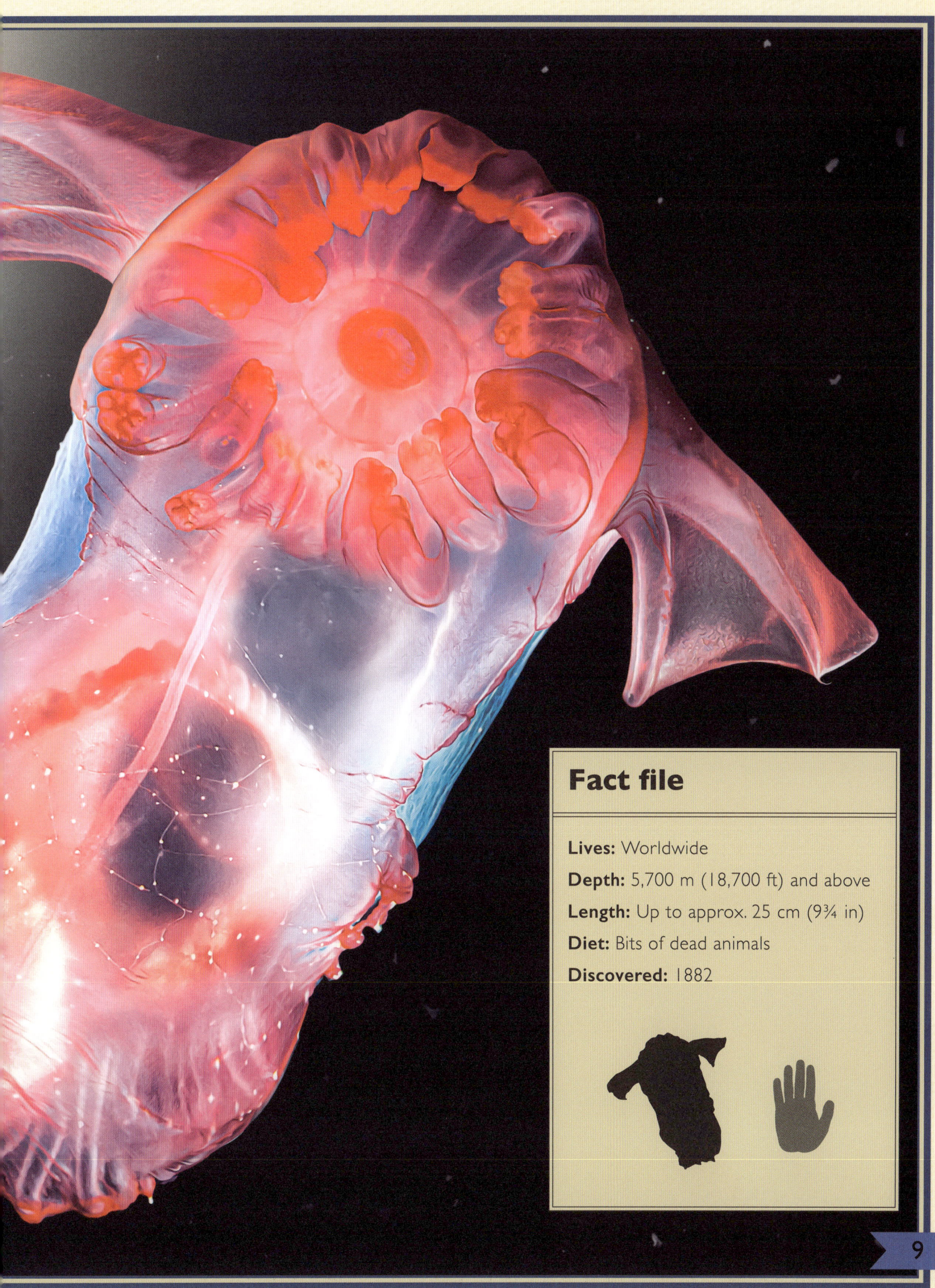

Fact file

Lives: Worldwide
Depth: 5,700 m (18,700 ft) and above
Length: Up to approx. 25 cm (9¾ in)
Diet: Bits of dead animals
Discovered: 1882

Vampire squid

Vampyroteuthis infernalis

- The vampire squid may sound menacing, but this is no bloodsucker — its dark, webbed arms look like a vampire cloak.

- A vampire squid has eight arms, which each have suckers. It also has two retractable sticky 'arms' called filaments for catching food. The squid uses small, finger-like spikes on the insides of its arms to scrape food off the filaments and push its meal into its mouth.

- This squid is an ancient ocean relic. Neither an octopus nor a true squid, a vampire squid is the only living animal of its kind.

- When threatened, a vampire squid can turn itself inside out. It pulls its arms up to show the spiky undersides of its webbed cloak. This is called the pineapple pose.

- This squid is covered in light-producing organs, and it uses them to scare off predators. It flashes the lights at the tip of each arm, and if it is under extreme threat can release a cloud of glowing goo into the water to confuse its enemy.

Fact file

Lives: Worldwide, except the poles
Depth: 600–900 m (1,950–2,950 ft)
Length: 30 cm (11¾ in)
Diet: Marine snow
Discovered: 1899

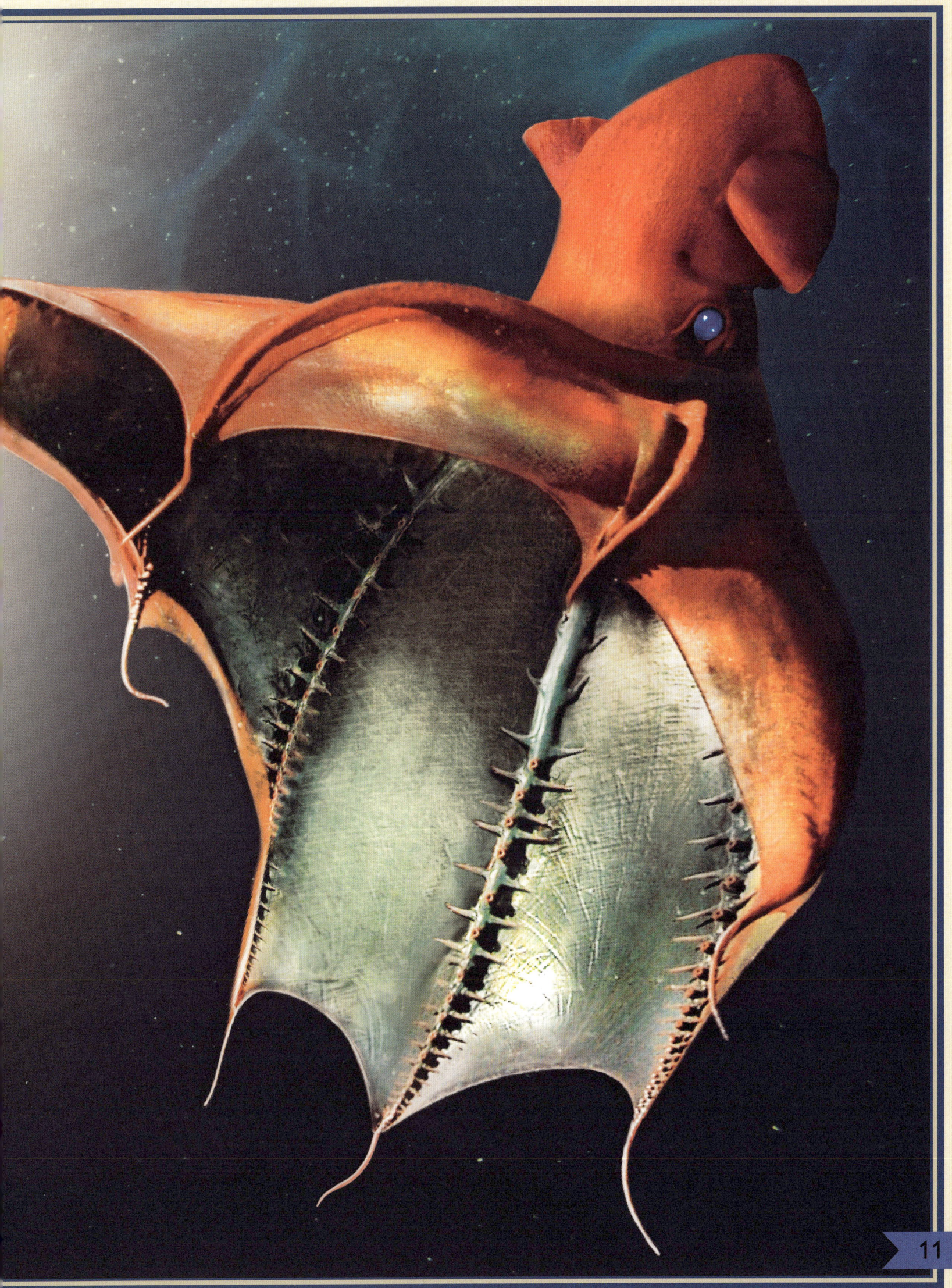

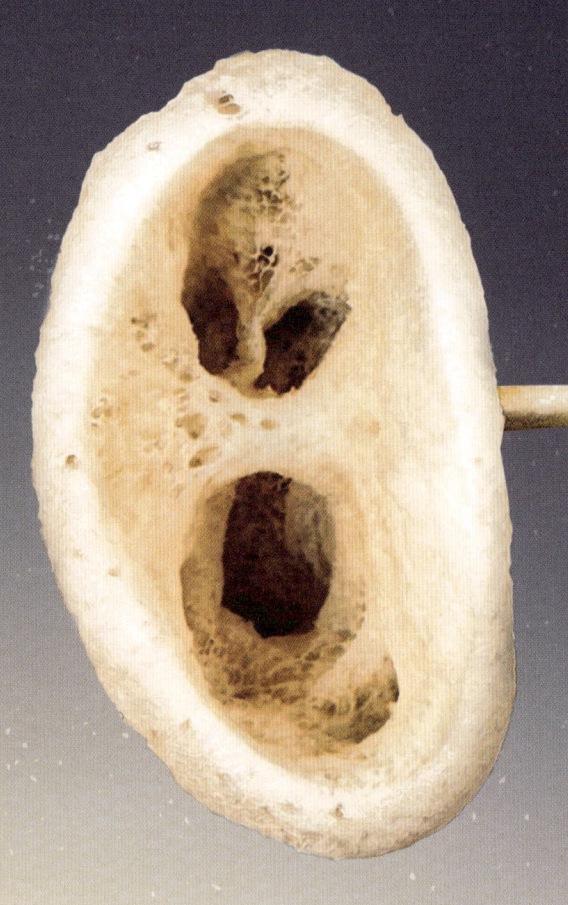

E.T. sponge

Advhena magnifica

- This odd-looking ocean dweller is the E.T. sponge. It is found in an area of the sea floor called the Forest of the Weird.

- The scientific name for the E.T. sponge is *Advhena magnifica*, which means 'magnificent alien' in Latin.

- The large openings on the sponge's body look like the big eyes of E.T., the loveable alien from the 1982 movie *E.T. the Extra-Terrestrial*. This is where this sponge gets its common name.

- A long stalk anchors the E.T. sponge to the seabed. Its body sits on top of the stalk where the current is stronger. The round openings in its body face the current so they can filter food from the water.

- The E.T. sponge is a type of glass sponge. Each one can live for thousands of years.

- Like all glass sponges, the E.T. sponge has a skeleton made partly of silica. This is the same material that makes up the glass in your windows.

Fact file

Lives: Pacific Ocean
Depth: 2,000 m (6,600 ft)
Length: Approx. 25 cm (9¾ in) including stalk
Diet: Plankton and bacteria
Discovered: 2016

Deep-sea siphonophore

Apolemia lanosa

 A deep-sea siphonophore (*sy-fon-o-for*) is not just one animal – it is many, many animals living together as one. Each animal is called a zooid and does a specific job. Some zooids swim, some eat and others digest food. None could live alone.

 At the beginning of its life, a deep-sea siphonophore is just one little egg. It grows by making tiny copies of itself, which all attach to the same stem.

 The siphonophore catches food by waiting for small floating animals to come into contact with its stinging tentacles. The prey is stunned, then pulled up into one of the siphonophore's many hungry mouths.

 Near one end of the siphonophore is a small, silvery, egg-shaped sac filled with gas. This helps the colony float and stops it from sinking into the murky ocean depths.

Fact file

Lives: Pacific Ocean
Depth: 600–1,800 m (1,950–5,900 ft)
Length: Up to 3 m (10 ft)
Diet: Zooplankton
Discovered: 2013

The clear section at the end of the siphonophore is called the nectosome. Zooids in the nectosome push out little jets of water to help the colony move.

 Siphonophores are the longest animals on Earth. Scientists found one that was a massive 46 metres (151 feet) long – that's nearly twice as long as an average blue whale!

Scaly-foot snail

Chrysomallon squamiferum

- The scaly-foot snail lives near hydrothermal vents – cracks in the sea floor that spew out hot water and minerals from Earth's core. The water surrounding a hydrothermal vent can reach 400°C (750°F).

- To protect its soft body from predators, the scaly-foot snail has a coiled shell, which is often covered in a dark layer of iron and sulphur. This iron coating acts like armour and makes the shell strong.

- Scaly-foot snails are endangered. Seabed mining threatens their deep-sea homes.

Fact file

Lives: Indian Ocean

Depth: 2,400–2,900 m (7,900–9,500 ft)

Length: Approx. 4.5 cm (1¾ in)

Diet: Chemicals turned into energy

Discovered: 2001

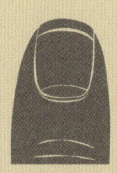

- The scaly-foot snail does not eat. Instead, the snail absorbs chemicals in the water near the hydrothermal vents where it lives through its gills, and bacteria in the snail's body turn these chemicals into energy.

- Not all scaly-foot snails look the same. Some are lighter coloured and do not have armoured shells covered in iron and sulphur.

- The bottom part of the scaly-foot snail's soft body is its foot, which it contracts and relaxes so it can move. The sides of the foot are protected by hundreds of small, tough scales, which are often strengthened by a coating of iron and sulphur.

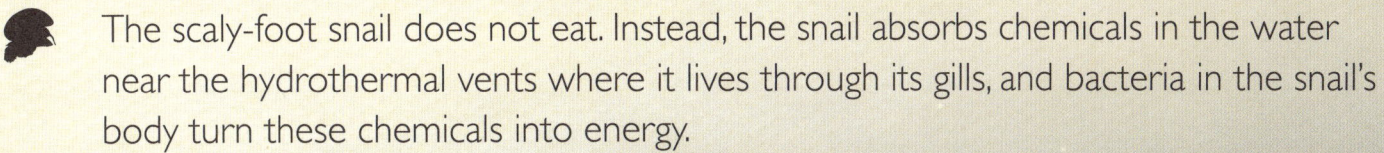

Shining bomber worm

Swima fulgida

- This deep-sea worm drops little bombs on its enemies. The bombs are small oval sacs that fall off when the worm is in trouble. They burst with bright green light to distract predators while the worm makes its escape.

- The shining bomber worm is blind – in fact, it does not even have eyes.

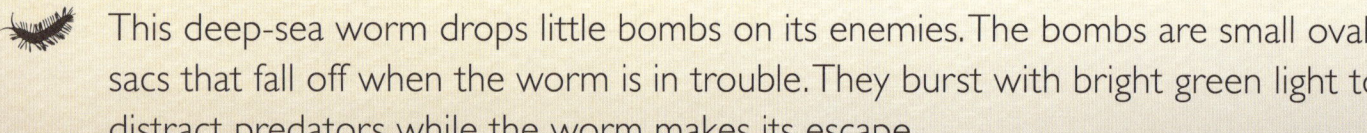

- The shining bomber worm has up to eight bombs attached to its head. Each time one explodes, its light lasts for a few seconds and then disappears. When a bomb is dropped, the worm can make another to replace the one it lost.

- An expert swimmer, the shining bomber worm can swim both forwards and backwards. It wiggles its shiny body and moves its bristles, which act like paddles to propel it through the water.

- When the shining bomber worm needs a rest, it floats in the water without sinking before continuing on its way.

- Most of the shining bomber worm's body is see-through, except for its dark grey and orange guts. These are visible through its skin.

Fact file

Lives: Pacific Ocean

Depth: 2,700–3,600 m (8,860–11,800 ft)

Length: Approx. 3 cm (1¼ in)

Diet: Unknown

Discovered: 2011

 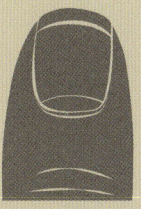

Deep-sea brittle star

Amphiodia spp.

- Brittle stars have a rounded body surrounded by long, slender arms. They are related to sea stars, or starfish.

- Most brittle stars have five arms. When threatened, they can drop an arm to distract predators and regrow it later.

- Brittle stars are sometimes called serpent stars because of their snake-like arms, which they use to pull themselves along the sea floor.

- Deep-sea brittle stars are energetic swimmers. Their winding arms flick back and forth like they are swimming breaststroke.

- If brittle stars lose an arm, they quickly figure out how to keep moving. Scientists are studying these creatures to learn how to build robots that keep working after they have been damaged.

- Some deep-sea brittle stars burrow into the sea floor and stick their arms up to catch floating bits of food. Others hunt small animals or eat carcasses.

- Brittle stars do not have eyes or brains, but they do have a mouth with five jaws.

- Some brittle stars flash green or blue light, probably to distract predators.

Fact file

Lives: Worldwide

Depth: 6,500 m (21,300 ft) and above

Length: Body up to 8 cm (3¼ in) across; arms up to 18 cm (7 in)

Diet: Zooplankton, dead animals

Discovered: 1860

Blob sculpin

Psychrolutes phrictus

- This deep-sea creature is a type of blobfish. It has a large head, big lips and widely spaced eyes. Its mouth curves down, almost as if it is frowning.

- The blob sculpin's skin is loose, flabby and mostly smooth, except for some fleshy bumps called cirri. These look a bit like spikes.

- There is not much muscle on a blob sculpin. Its fatty flesh weighs slightly less than water, so it can swim along near the sea floor without sinking or floating up.

- This blobfish lays nests full of pink eggs. It cares for the eggs by sitting on them and fanning them to keep them clean.

- Blob sculpins build their nests close to each other. Scientists once discovered 64 nests at one site, some of them just 1 metre (3 feet) apart.

- The blob sculpin does not have teeth. It sucks in any food that floats in front of it.

Fact file

Lives: Pacific Ocean
Depth: 2,800 m (9,200 ft) and above
Length: Up to 70 cm (2 ft 3½ in)
Diet: Sea pens, snails, crabs and other small prey
Discovered: 1978

Gulper eel

Eurypharynx pelecanoides

- The gulper eel has a long, thin body, a tail like a whip and a huge mouth that can be nearly a quarter of the eel's total length.

- When it feeds, a gulper eel sucks in seawater along with its prey, leaving its mouth puffed up like a water balloon. To deflate its mouth to normal size, it first swallows its food whole and then pushes the water out through its gills.

- This eel is not a fussy eater. It will feed on small crustaceans, fish and squid, and it will also eat seaweed when it comes across it.

- A gulper eel is also called a pelican eel because of how it feeds. Like a pelican, this eel scoops prey into its mouth along with a lot of seawater.

- Male gulper eels have a better sense of smell than females. This helps them to find a mate.

- On the tip of a gulper eel's tail is a light organ that can flash pink or red. This may be a trick to attract prey, although scientists do not yet know for sure.

Fact file

Lives: Worldwide, except the poles
Depth: 3,000 m (9,850 ft) and above
Length: Up to 1 m (3 ft)
Diet: Crustaceans, fish, squid
Discovered: 1882

25

Humpback anglerfish

Melanocetus johnsonii

- The female humpback anglerfish is famous for the shining lantern, or lure, on the top of her head. She uses the light to trick prey into coming close enough to capture in her gaping jaw.

- An anglerfish's lure lights up thanks to the tiny glowing bacteria that live there. In exchange for their light, the bacteria are protected from predators.

- The fishing pole-like structure that sticks out of the head of a female humpback anglerfish is really a type of fin.

- This anglerfish is sometimes called a black sea devil because of its dark, monstrous appearance.

Fact file

Lives: Worldwide
Depth: 300–2,500 m (980–8,200 ft)
Length: Up to 18 cm (7 in)
Diet: Crustaceans and small fish
Discovered: 1863

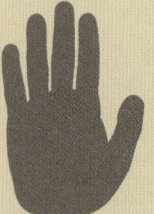

- 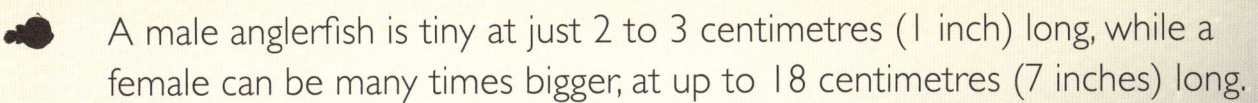 A male anglerfish is tiny at just 2 to 3 centimetres (1 inch) long, while a female can be many times bigger, at up to 18 centimetres (7 inches) long.

- 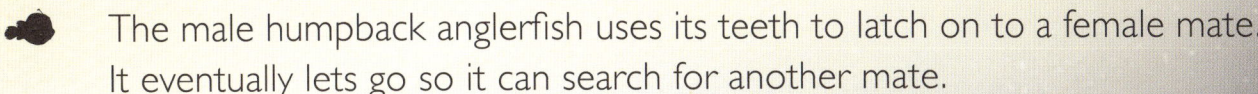 The male humpback anglerfish uses its teeth to latch on to a female mate. It eventually lets go so it can search for another mate.

Giant tubeworm

Riftia pachyptila

- Each of these red-and-white creatures is a giant tubeworm. The white tubes are their hard outer skeletons, and the red, feathery parts are gills. Tubeworms can pull the gills inside the tubes and close the openings to protect themselves from predators.

- The giant tubeworm lives deep in the Pacific Ocean near cracks in the sea floor. These are called hydrothermal vents and they spew out super-hot water and toxic chemicals that reach up to 400° C (750° F).

- The tubeworm does not eat food like most animals do, and it does not make energy from sunlight like a plant, either. Bacteria living inside the giant tubeworm's body turn chemicals in the water into the energy the worm needs to survive.

- A giant tubeworm's feathery gills look red because they are filled with red blood.

Fact file

Lives: Pacific Ocean

Depth: 1,900–3,600 m (6,250–11,800 ft)

Length: Up to approx. 2 m (6½ ft)

Diet: Chemicals turned into energy

Discovered: 1977

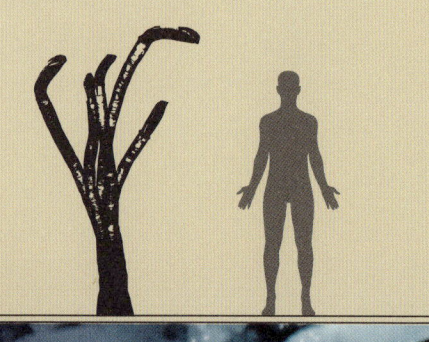

Scientists once found a huge group of giant tubeworms and named the area the Rose Garden, because the worms looked like long-stemmed roses growing out of the sea floor.

Goblin shark

Mitsukurina owstoni

- The goblin shark cannot chase speedy prey. Instead, it thrusts fast-moving jaws attached to stretchy flaps of skin right out of its mouth. The jaws snatch the prey before it swims away. The shark then pulls its jaws back in, along with its meal.

- Small holes, or pores, along the goblin shark's long, flat snout sense prey and help the shark to hunt in the dark.

- The goblin shark looks slightly pink because its blood vessels show through its skin. Baby goblin sharks are nearly white, but their skin darkens as they grow.

- Often seen off the coast of Japan, this shark is named for its similarity to a long-nosed goblin-like creature from Japanese folklore.

- The goblin shark has super-sharp front teeth and smaller, flattened teeth at the back. The back teeth may help the shark crush its prey before swallowing.

- Human rubbish has been found in the stomachs of some goblin sharks. They sometimes mistake this waste for food.

Fact file

Lives: Worldwide, except the poles

Depth: 1,300 m (4,250 ft)

Length: Up to 4 m (13 ft)

Diet: Fish, squid, octopuses, crustaceans

Discovered: 1898

Sparks' two-armed ctenophore

Duobrachium sparksae

- The Sparks' two-armed ctenophore (teen-oh-for) is a type of comb jelly. A comb jelly's body is made up almost completely of water. It has no bones, no brain, no heart and no blood.

- This ctenophore can extend its tentacles up to seven times the length of its body. When not stretched out, the tentacles are coiled up inside the animal's two arms.

- The end of each of the ctenophore's two retractable arms are covered by mini tentacles that are smaller than grains of rice. These mini tentacles are called tentilla, and they are probably used for catching small prey.

- Instead of a brain, this comb jelly has a network of nerves that helps it sense and interact with its environment.

- When scientists found this comb jelly, it appeared to be using its long tentacles to anchor itself to the sea floor and looked like a balloon with two strings.

- Like other comb jellies, this species uses the rows of 'combs' that run along its body to swim. When a deep-sea submarine shines light on the combs, they split the light into the colours of the rainbow.

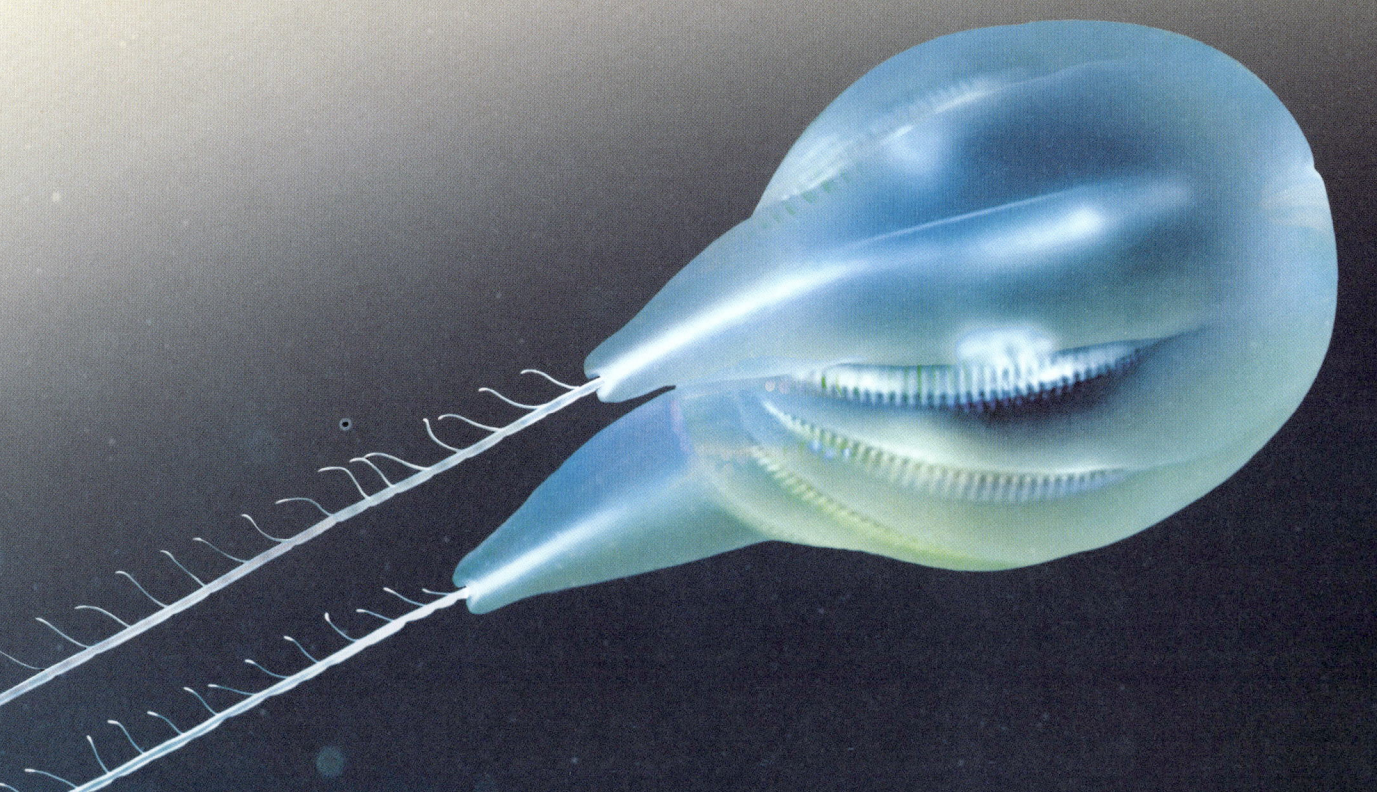

Fact file

Lives: Atlantic Ocean

Depth: 3,900 m (12,800 ft)

Length: Body up to 8 cm (3¼ in); extended tentacles 30–56 cm (1 ft–1 ft 10 in)

Diet: Zooplankton

Discovered: 2015

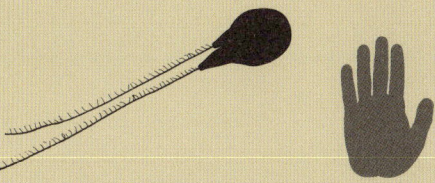

Black swallower

Chiasmodon niger

- The black swallower is a predator that eats its prey in one gulp. Its balloon-like stomach even allows it to swallow prey more than twice the swallower's length.

- After swallowing a large fish, the black swallower's body digests its big meal very slowly. While doing so, it will not hunt for more food.

- A baby black swallower looks very different to an adult. It has little spikes on its head and body, is lighter in colour and has spots that disappear as it grows.

- This deep-sea fish has curved, backward-facing teeth that are designed to trap prey inside its mouth and throat.

- An adult black swallower is dark brown or black with a slightly lighter belly. The skin on its stomach can stretch to the point that it becomes almost see-through.

- As young fish, black swallowers live closer to the surface at up to 1,000 metres (3,300 feet) deep. Adults live up to 3,900 metres (12,800 feet) down.

Fact file

Lives: Atlantic Ocean

Depth: 730–3,900 m (2,400–12,800 ft)

Length: Up to 25 cm (9¾ in)

Diet: Other fish

Discovered: 1864

Giant isopod

Bathynomus giganteus

- There is not a lot to eat in the cold, deep waters where giant isopods live. This creature must rely on marine snow – tiny flakes of fish droppings and bits of dead animals that drift down from the ocean surface.

- A giant isopod looks similar to an enormous woodlouse – and for a good reason. The two species are related.

- An isopod has a tough outer shell. When threatened, it can roll itself into a ball to protect its soft underside. Most predators will not prey on a giant isopod, though. It is tough to eat and not very meaty.

Fact file

Lives: Pacific and Atlantic Oceans
Depth: 170–2,100 m (560–6,900 ft)
Length: Up to 50 cm (1 ft 7¾ in)
Diet: Marine snow, crabs, small fish, whale carcasses
Discovered: 1879

- Shine a light on this mysterious creature and its eyes seem to glow. This is because the giant isopod's triangular eyes reflect light.

- Because giant isopods do not know when they will next come across food, they store energy as fat in their livers. This energy is used slowly and sparingly.

- In addition to 14 legs and a fan-like tail, a giant isopod has four antennae and two pairs of swimming legs called pleopods.

- If a giant isopod cannot find food, it can go for years without a single meal.

- Scientists found plastic in the stomachs of three giant isopods. This suggests that humans affect even the deepest parts of the ocean and the creatures that live there.

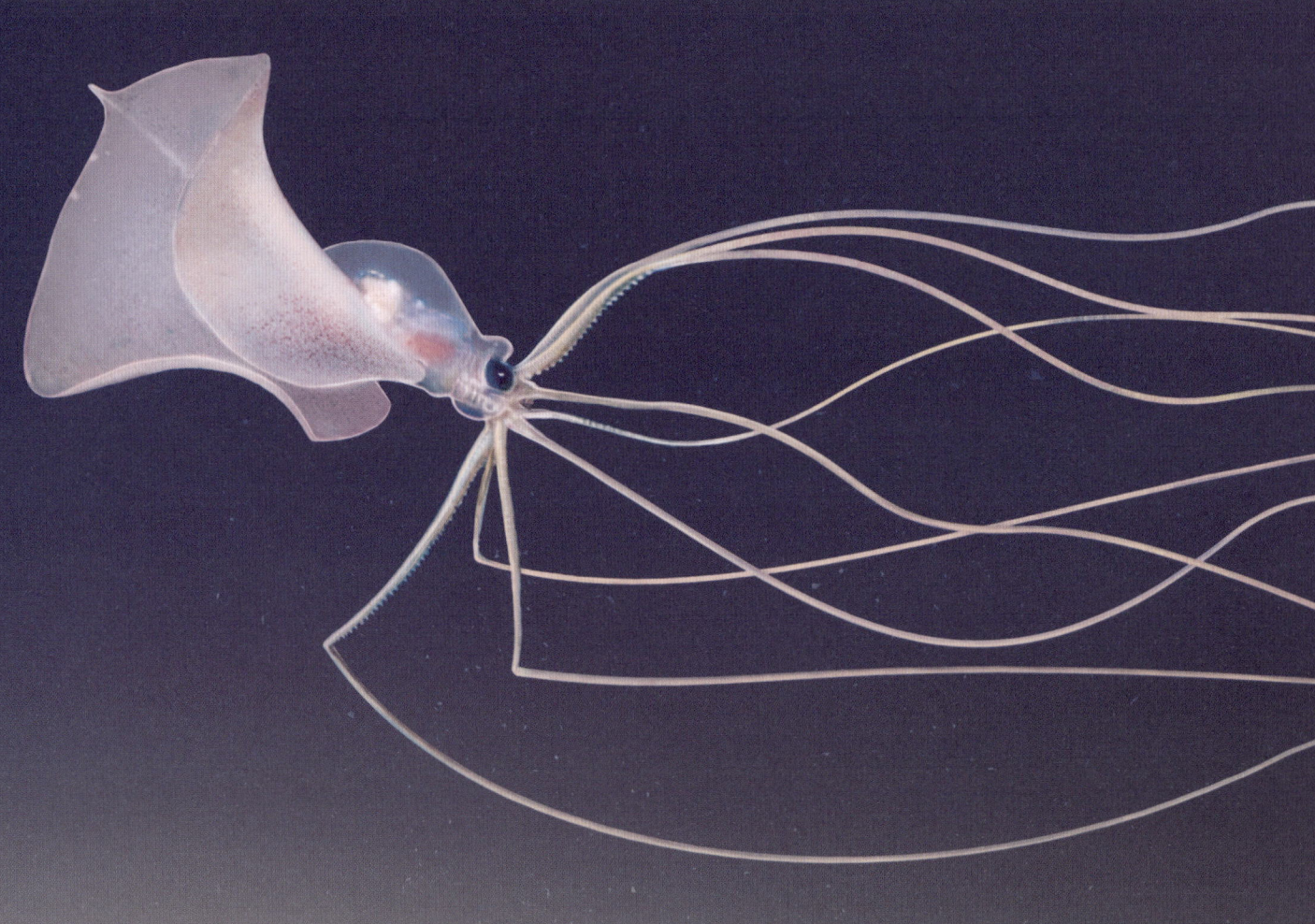

Bigfin squid

Magnapinna spp.

- The bigfin squid is named after the large fin on the top of its head, which helps it swim. Its long, spaghetti-like arms and tentacles give the animal another nickname – the long-armed squid.

- Unlike most squids, the bigfin squid's eight arms and two tentacles are all the same length. It may be able to change the length of its arms and tentacles by drawing them in and extending them out.

- Tiny suckers cover the bigfin squid's arms and tentacles. They are probably used to help it catch prey.

- This squid holds the top part of its arms straight out from its body, dangling the bottom part of its arms downwards. This is known as elbow pose because it looks like the squid has elbows.

- The bigfin squid sometimes floats horizontally just above the sea floor. Scientists are not yet sure why.

No one knows for certain what bigfin squid eat or how they capture food. They may drag their arms and tentacles across the sea floor looking for prey, or they may use their arms like a spider's web to trap food.

Fact file

Lives: Atlantic and Pacific Oceans
Depth: 4,735 m (15,535 ft) and above
Length: Up to 8 m (26¼ ft)
Diet: Unknown, probably zooplankton
Discovered: 1998

Tripod fish

Bathypterois grallator

- This tripod fish is on the hunt for food. It perches on its three stilt-like fins and faces the slow current, waiting for food to drift past.

- The fins of a tripod fish can grow to over 1 metre (3 feet) long. That's nearly three times the size of its body!

- The tripod fish does not have good eyesight. Instead, when searching for food, it relies on its fins to find prey by sensing nearby vibrations in the water.

- When it swims, the tripod fish relaxes its fins so they trail behind it. When it lands back on the sea floor, they become stiff enough for it to stand on them.

- The tripod fish has tiny pads on its three long fins. These keep the fish from sinking into the sand or mud when perching on the sea floor.

- If this fish cannot find a mate to reproduce, it can do so on its own. This is because it has both male and female parts.

Fact file

Lives: Worldwide, except the poles
Depth: 900–4,700 m (2,950–15,400 ft)
Length: Up to 43 cm (1 ft 5 in)
Diet: Zooplankton
Discovered: 1886

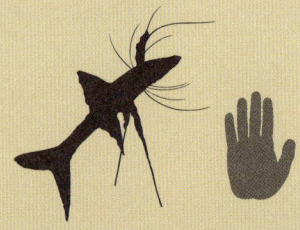

Barreleye

Macropinna microstoma

- The top of a barreleye's head is completely see-through. This allows it to spot prey swimming right above it. Its large eyes can also move to look forwards, which helps the fish catch the prey in its tiny mouth.

- This deep-sea fish has bright green, barrel-shaped eyes that are entirely inside its head. It is the shape of the eyes that give the barreleye its name.

- The barreleye's fluid-filled head acts as a shield to protect its eyes from the stings of the jellyfish it eats.

- The two holes above a barreleye's mouth may look like eyes, but they are really fish nostrils called nares. They are used for smelling rather than breathing.

- Most of a barreleye's time is spent floating motionless in the water, gazing up and using its big fins to steady itself. It waits and watches for the silhouettes of possible prey.

- Barreleyes steal food from animals called siphonophores. They carefully swim among the siphonophore's stinging tentacles, picking off the creatures that have been captured.

Fact file

Lives: Pacific Ocean
Depth: 600–800 m (1,950–2,600 ft)
Length: 15 cm (6 in)
Diet: Zooplankton, including jellyfish
Discovered: 1939

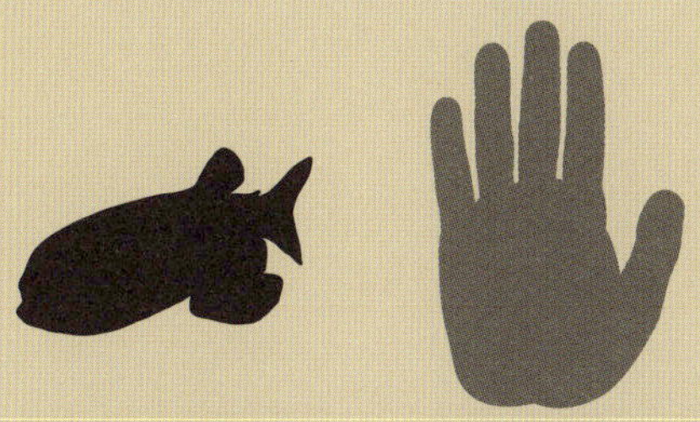

Giant deep-sea nudibranch

Bathydoris aioca

- The giant deep-sea nudibranch (*nu-dee-brank*) lives on the soft, sandy sea floor off the coast of North America.

- Nudibranchs are marine snails that lose their shells when they become adults. They come in many shapes, sizes and colours.

- The two ear-like spikes on the giant deep-sea nudibranch's head are called rhinophores. They are more like nostrils than ears because they help the animal search for food.

- A nudibranch uses the tiny teeth on its radula, which is similar to a tongue, to break down its food.

- The giant deep-sea nudibranch is blind. In fact, it does not have eyes.

- The name nudibranch means 'naked gill'. Nudibranchs do not have gills like a fish's. Some have feathery gills on their outsides, such as on the tops or backsides of their body, and others breathe through their skin.

- This round sea creature moves along the sea floor using the slimy, muscular foot on the bottom of its body.

Fact file

Lives: Pacific Ocean
Depth: 3,300 m (10,800 ft) and above
Length: Approx. 30 cm (11 ¾ in)
Diet: Unknown
Discovered: 1962

Common fangtooth

Anoplogaster cornuta

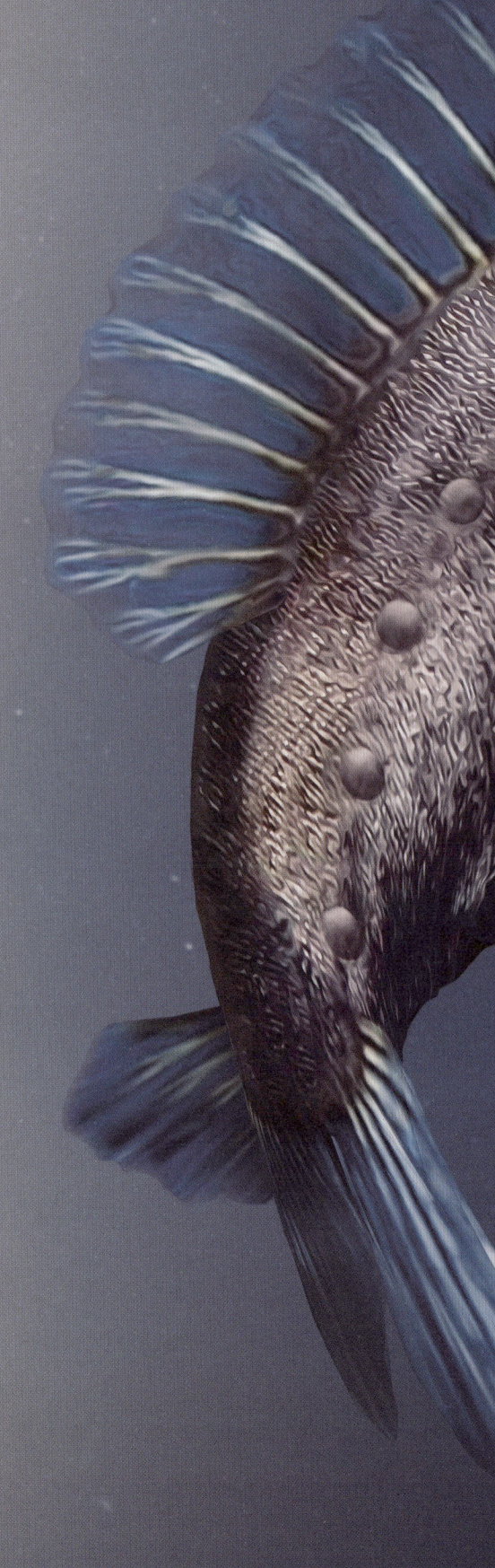

- This deep-sea fish is only about the size of a small banana. Its big mouth and sharp fangs help it snatch its dinner – often a shrimp or fish.

- A fangtooth's lower fangs fit into special pockets in its upper jaw. If there were no pockets, the fish would pierce its own brain when it closed its mouth.

- The common fangtooth has very dark skin. Scientists call this skin ultra-black because it only reflects a tiny bit of light. This keeps the fangtooth hidden from bigger predators in the dark ocean.

- The common fangtooth cannot see very well, but the long grooves down the sides of its body help it sense movement in the water. These alert it to possible nearby prey.

- Pockets of mucus dot the common fangtooth's face. It is a mystery what the fish uses them for.

- A young common fangtooth looks different to an adult. It is grey instead of black or brown, has spines on its head and only has tiny teeth. The sharp fangs grow as it gets older.

Fact file

Lives: Worldwide, except poles
Depth: 5,000 m (16,400 ft) and above
Length: Up to 18 cm (7 in)
Diet: Crustaceans, squid, fish
Discovered: 1833

Emperor dumbo octopus

Grimpoteuthis imperator

- This dumbo octopus was named 'emperor' after the underwater mountain range where it was found – the Hawaiian-Emperor seamount chain.

- Many octopuses squirt a blue-black ink to help them escape from predators. The dumbo octopus does not do that because a dark ink is not visible in the deep parts of the ocean where it lives.

- This octopus is called a dumbo because the fins on its head look like the giant ears on the flying elephant from the Disney film *Dumbo*. It glides through the murky ocean depths by flapping these fins.

Fact file

Lives: Pacific Ocean

Depth: 3,900–4,400 m (12,800–14,450 ft)

Size: 30–50 cm (11¾ in–1 ft 7¾ in)

Diet: Worms, amphipods, copepods, and other small animals

Discovered: 2016

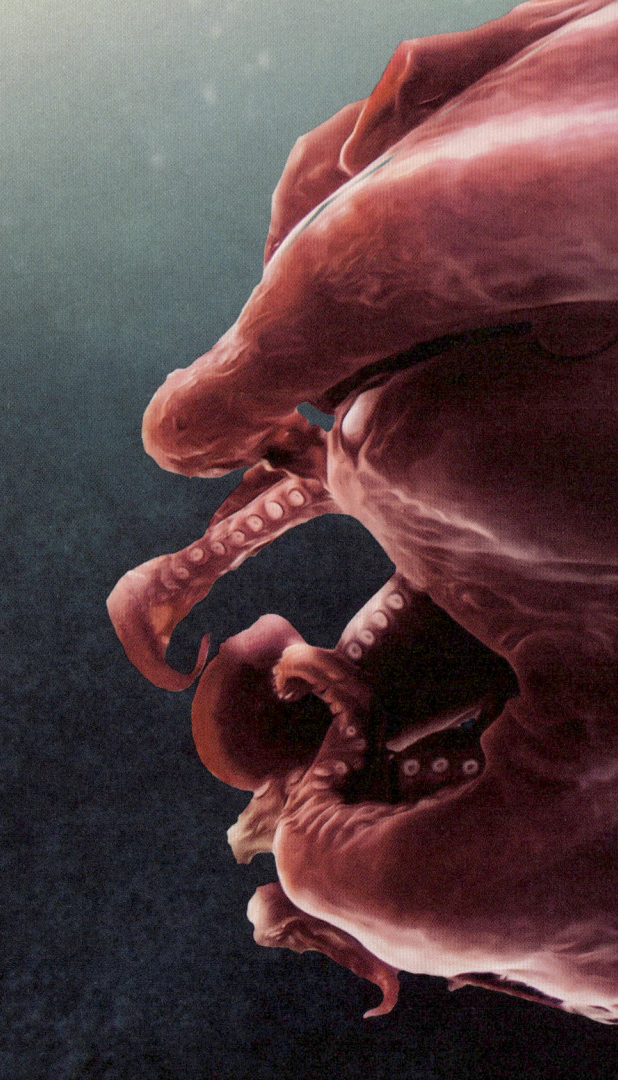

- There are hundreds of different types of octopuses, and at least 15 species of dumbo octopuses. Dumbos live deeper in the ocean than any other octopus group.

- The dumbo octopus is a hunter. Its prey includes worms and tiny shrimp-like creatures. The octopus hovers over the sea floor and, when it sees something tasty, swoops in and swallows it whole.

Whalefish

Gyrinomimus grahami

- A female whalefish's wide body and big mouth make it look like a miniature baleen whale, which is how it got its name. The female is about five times bigger than a male whalefish.

- Scientists once thought that baby whalefish, male whalefish and female whalefish were three totally different animals. The babies were called tapetails and the males were called bignoses. Females have always been known as whalefish.

- An adult male whalefish does not eat. In fact, its jaws cannot open. While it is young, a male whalefish gorges itself on small crustaceans and can survive on what is in its stomach for the rest of its adult life.

- Adult whalefish are reddish orange. This colour acts as camouflage because red and orange look black in the deep sea.

- The female whalefish has tiny eyes and very poor eyesight. It finds food by feeling vibrations in the water using holes on its head and body.

- A baby whalefish looks nothing like an adult whalefish. As well as being tiny, it has a long tail that can be even longer than its body.

Fact file

Lives: Worldwide, except the Arctic Ocean

Depth: 1,500–3,500 m (4,900–11,500 ft)

Length: 40 cm (1 ft 3¾ in)

Diet: Males do not eat; females eat crustaceans and fish

Discovered: 1964

Zombie worm

Osedax spp.

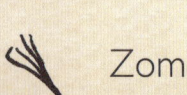 Zombie worms eat the bones of dead animals. Thousands of these worms can cover a skeleton resting on the sea floor. They move in after other animals have eaten everything but the dead creature's bones.

 A female zombie worm does not have a mouth or a stomach. To eat, it roots itself into a bone, then dissolves the bone with acid. Bacteria living inside the worm turn the dissolved bone into energy it uses to live.

Male zombie worms are tiny compared to females. In fact, they live inside the females, which can have more than a hundred inside them at any time. Larger females usually host more males.

 The reddish top part of a zombie worm is called the crown. This is attached to a part of the worm's body called the trunk, which joins roots that bury into animal bone for food.

 Scientists know about more than 25 species of zombie worms, and there are probably many more waiting to be discovered.

Fact file

Lives: Worldwide

Depth: Up to 3,000 m (9,850 ft)

Length: Females up to 7 cm (2¾ in); males 1 mm (0.04 in)

Diet: Bones, especially whale bones

Discovered: 2002

Sea pig

Scotoplanes globosa

- A sea pig is a type of sea cucumber that lives on the deep seabed. It spends its time digging for food in the mud using the tentacles around its mouth.

- This creature walks on top of the soft, muddy sea floor using its tube-like feet. There are four more feet on top of its body, which look like antennae. Scientists are not sure what these upper feet are used for, but they may help the animal find food.

- The sea pig's body is see-through and can range in colour from pink to purple.

Fact file

Lives: Worldwide

Depth: 550–6,700 m (1,800–22,000 ft)

Length: Up to 16.5 cm (6½ in)

Diet: Bits of dead animals

Discovered: 1879

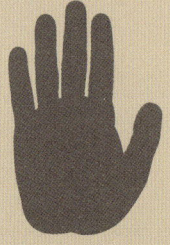

- Sea pigs are one of the most common animals on the deep-sea floor. Scientists sometimes find them in big groups, or herds.

- The sea pig will eat just about anything — including bits of dead animals and animal droppings.

- This deep-sea creature sometimes carries young king crabs on its back or belly. No one knows exactly why, but ocean scientists think the crabs cling to the sea pig for protection against predators.

Owlfish

Pseudobathylagus milleri

- Just like an owl's big eyes help it hunt at night, the owlfish's large eyes allow it to spot predators and prey in the deep, dark sea where it lives.

- An owlfish uses its tiny mouth to eat small sea creatures called zooplankton, such as crustaceans and sea jellies.

- The owlfish swims slowly through the ocean as it watches for prey. If it needs to make a quick escape from a predator, it can dart away with a flick of its forked tail.

- This fish's dark scales help it blend into its murky deep-sea habitat.

- If a predator such as a squid attacks an owlfish, the fish can shed some of its large scales to help escape its attacker's grip. The scales grow back over time.

- The owlfish is a type of fish called a smelt. It is also known as the stout blacksmelt or the bigscaled blacksmelt.

Fact file

Lives: Pacific Ocean
Depth: 550–6,600 m (1,800–21,650 ft)
Length: Up to 21.6 cm (8½ in)
Diet: Zooplankton
Discovered: 1898

Sperm whale

Physeter macrocephalus

- This ocean giant is one of the deepest divers on Earth. It dives thousands of metres and stays underwater for well over an hour before surfacing to breathe.

- The sperm whale hunts squid in the ocean depths. Scientists have found giant squid beaks in sperm whale stomachs and scars left on their skin from squid suckers.

- To hunt in the deep where there is no light, a sperm whale makes high-pitched clicks that echo off nearby objects. The echoes tell the whale where everything is, including possible food.

- The sperm whale has the largest brain of any animal on Earth, weighing nearly 9 kilograms (20 pounds).

- An oily liquid fills a sperm whale's giant head. Humans once hunted these animals for the oil, which they used to light lamps and make candles. Today, it is illegal to hunt whales and sell whale oil.

- The sperm whale has the biggest teeth of any whale. But it has such tiny top teeth that they do not usually even break through the whale's upper gums.

Fact file

Lives: Worldwide

Depth: 3,050 m (10,000 ft) and above

Length: Up to 18 m (60 ft)

Diet: Large and medium-sized squid, fish, sharks

Discovered: 1758

Bloodybelly comb jelly

Lampocteis cruentiventer

- This blood-red, deep-sea creature is not a jellyfish – it is a comb jelly. Unlike jellyfish, comb jellies do not sting.

- Comb jellies have oval-shaped bodies and eight rows of hair-like cilia. The cilia look like multicoloured combs and act like tiny paddles to help the comb jellies swim.

- When light shines on the hair-like cilia on a bloodybelly comb jelly's body, they appear rainbow coloured. This is because the cilia split light into the colours of the rainbow, allowing us to see them all.

- A bloodybelly comb jelly's droppings look like a trail of sparkles. A comb jelly takes food in at one end of its body and ejects waste out of the other end.

Fact file

Lives: Pacific Ocean

Depth: 2,000 m (6,600 ft) and above

Length: Up to 16 cm (6¼ in)

Diet: Zooplankton

Discovered: 1979

- Bloodybelly comb jellies' bellies are dark red. This is because red is nearly impossible to see in the deep sea, so this colour helps the jelly hide in the dark – even if it has eaten something that glows.

- This jelly has larger, brighter comb rows than most other comb jellies. Its scientific name *Lampocteis* comes from the Greek words for 'bright' and 'combs'.

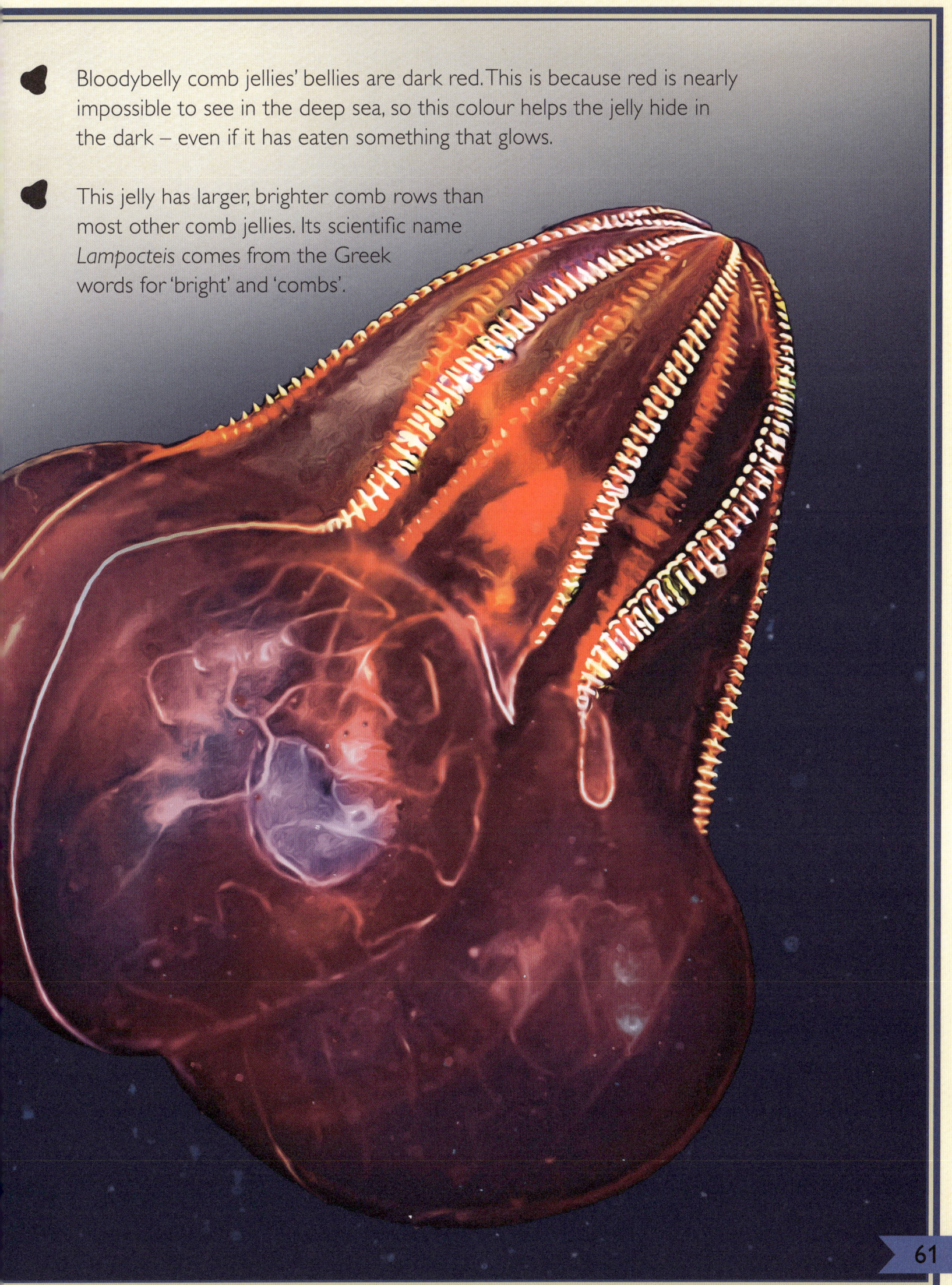

Mariana snailfish

Pseudoliparis swirei

- The Mariana snailfish may be the deepest-living fish in the ocean. Scientists discovered it in the Mariana Trench, which is the deepest place in the world.

- This fish has tiny eyes and weak eyesight. It may even be blind. Because there is no light far down in the ocean where the Mariana snailfish lives, it does not rely on its sight to survive.

- Small crustaceans called hadal amphipods are an important part of this snailfish's diet. It inflates its stomach to cram in as many of these little creatures as possible.

- The Mariana snailfish's bones are softer than those of most other fish. This makes the bones more flexible and helps them handle the extreme pressure of all that seawater down in the deepest parts of the planet.

- Nothing hunts this snailfish in the Mariana Trench, making it the top predator there. It has its choice of the food available.

- The Mariana snailfish is partly see-through. Its stomach, liver and other organs can be seen through its pinkish-white skin.

Fact file

Lives: Pacific Ocean
Depth: 8,075 m (26,500 ft) and above
Length: 10–29 cm (4–11½ in)
Diet: Amphipods and other small animals
Discovered: 2014

Dandelion siphonophore

Thermopalia taraxaca

- The dandelion siphonophore (*sy-fon-oh-for*) is a colony of animals living together as one. Each part of this yellow-orange ball is a separate animal called a zooid, with a special job that keeps the colony alive.

- Most siphonophores spend their lives floating and swimming. But dandelion siphonophores often anchor themselves to the sea floor with their long feeding tentacles.

- A siphonophore's feeding tentacles have tiny stinging cells that inject deadly venom into their captured prey.

- The brown, worm-like parts of the dandelion siphonophore are the zooids that eat and digest food.

Fact file

Lives: Pacific Ocean

Depth: 2,480–2,940 m (8,140–9,650 ft)

Length: Body approx. 5 cm (2 in)

Diet: Plankton

Discovered: 1977

- A dandelion siphonophore hatches from an egg and looks like a long, oval sac. As it grows, one end forms a float. The sac lengthens to form a stem from which the colony of zooids grows.

- Scientists found this creature near hydrothermal vents, or cracks in the sea floor, in 1977. They thought it looked like a dandelion flower, so they gave it a name that means 'dandelion from the hot sea-vent hole'.

Strawberry squid

Histioteuthis heteropsis

- This squid gets its name from its pinky-red colour and the dots on its body, which look like strawberry seeds.

- The dots on a strawberry squid's body are light organs called photophores. The photophores light up just enough to match the amount of light around the squid, so it blends in without creating a shadow.

- The strawberry squid has a big eye and a small eye to help it look for prey. One eye watches the waters above the squid, while the other focuses its gaze below. The big eye is yellow and can be twice the size of the small eye.

- This squid rests at a slight angle so its eyes can point in different directions. The big eye captures as much as light as possible to help the strawberry squid see the shadows of predators or prey swimming above it. The small eye watches for the flashing lights of creatures below it.

- A young strawberry squid looks more pink than red, and its eyes are both small. As it grows, one eye gets big and the other stays small.

- When in danger, a strawberry squid may release an ink cloud about the same size and shape as its own body. This tricks a predator into thinking the ink cloud is the squid itself.

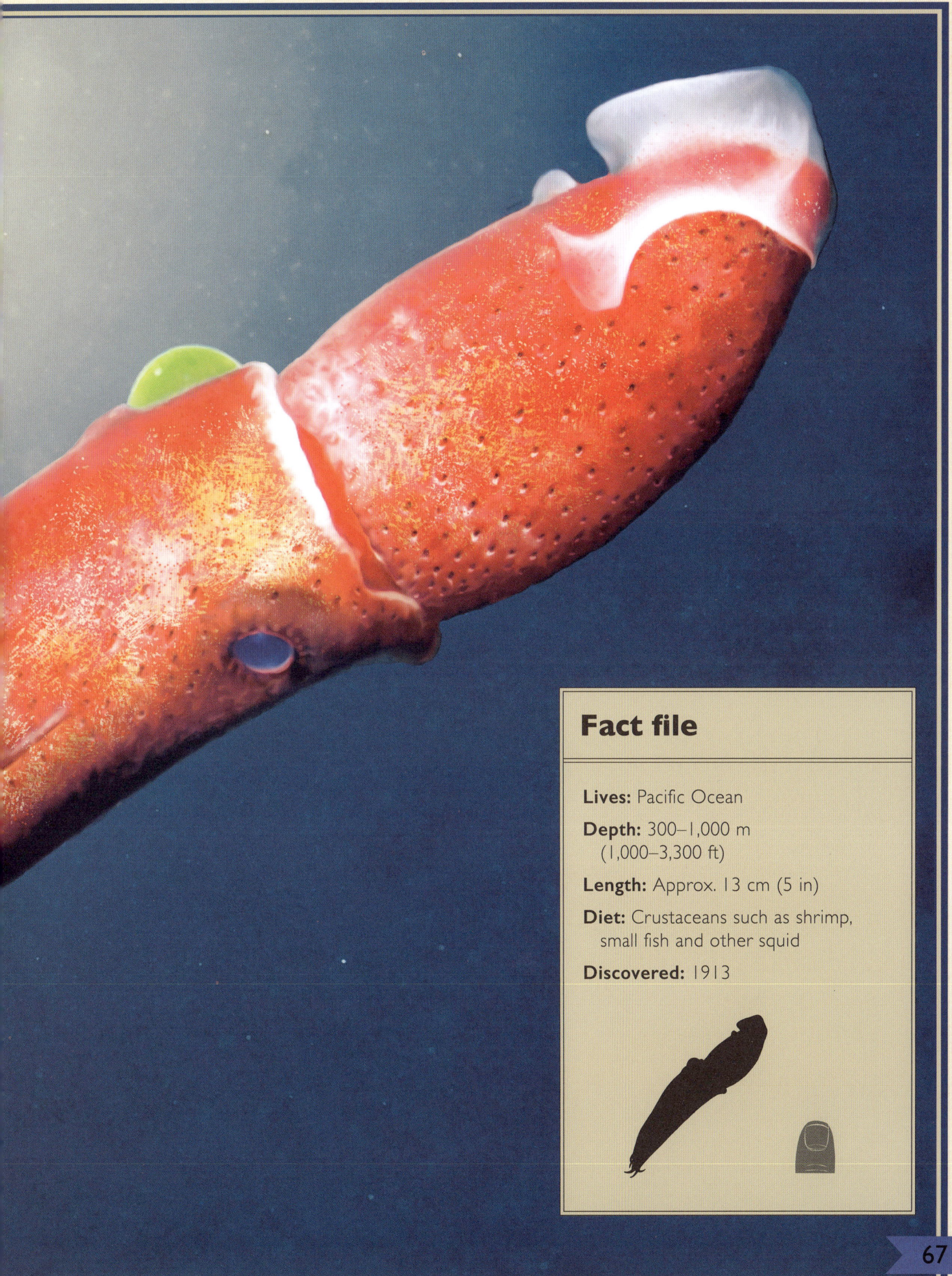

Fact file

Lives: Pacific Ocean

Depth: 300–1,000 m (1,000–3,300 ft)

Length: Approx. 13 cm (5 in)

Diet: Crustaceans such as shrimp, small fish and other squid

Discovered: 1913

Greenland shark

Somniosus microcephalus

- Greenland sharks can live to be hundreds of years old – possibly 500. They do not reach adulthood until they have lived for well over a century.

- This slow-moving deep-sea shark swims at less than 3 kilometres per hour (2 miles per hour). That's slower than an average person walks.

- Greenland sharks hunt fish, crustaceans and seals. The sharks probably capture seals by carefully sneaking up on them as they sleep underwater. These sharks will also eat dead animals that sink down from the surface, including polar bears and seabirds.

- Female Greenland sharks are pregnant for eight years, or possibly even longer, before giving birth to a litter of pups. They can have hundreds of pups during their long lifetimes.

- Greenland shark meat is poisonous to humans, but that has not protected the sharks from human harm. People have hunted these animals for centuries for the oil in their livers.

- Tiny creatures called copepods often latch onto Greenland sharks' eyeballs. The copepods ruin the sharks' vision and can eventually cause them blindness.

Fact file

Lives: North Atlantic and Arctic Oceans

Depth: 2,990 m (9,800 ft) and above

Length: Up to 7.3 m (24 ft)

Diet: Fish, seals, crustaceans, dead animals

Discovered: 1801

Giant phantom jelly

Stygiomedusa gigantea

- A giant phantom jelly is a giant indeed. Its bell head is about 1 metre (3 feet) across, and its four curtain-like arms can be more than 10 metres (30 feet) long.

- Instead of stinging its prey, the giant phantom jelly uses its long arms to capture prey and start digesting it.

- This ghostly ocean giant is a deep reddish-brown or plum colour. This makes it nearly invisible in the deep because shades of red are hard to see so far down.

- This jelly often lives alongside a deep-sea fish called the pelagic brotula. The fish hovers by the jelly's head, or bell, and hides within its ribbon-like arms for protection.

- The giant phantom jelly feeds on tiny creatures called plankton. To make sure it has a reliable food supply, the jelly travels to places where lots of plankton are found, such as cracks in the sea floor called hydrothermal vents.

- A female giant phantom jelly gives birth to live young. Baby giant phantom jellies look like tiny copies of the adults.

Fact file

Lives: Worldwide, except the Arctic

Depth: 6665 m (21,870 ft) and above

Length: Head approx 1 m (3 ft) across; arms 10 m (30 ft)

Diet: Plankton and small fish

Discovered: 1899

Pom-pom anemone

Liponema brevicorne

- Pom-pom anemones are also called tumbleweed anemones. This is because they sometimes roll across the sea floor like tumbleweed in the desert. They are pushed along by deep-sea currents and do not stop until they run into something solid.

- Most of the time, pom-pom anemones attach themselves to the sea floor, catching passing food with their stinging tentacles.

- Pom-pom anemones can let tentacles drop off if a predator is attacking them. Like most anemones, they are able to regrow any lost tentacles.

Fact file

Lives: Pacific Ocean

Depth: 3,000 m (9,850 ft) and above

Length: Up to 25 cm (9¾ in)

Diet: Plankton, krill and other small crustaceans

Discovered: 1893

- Scientists have found pom-pom anemones in the deepest part of the ocean near hydrothermal vents – places where hot water spews out of cracks in the sea floor. They also tend to collect near dead whales that sink to the bottom of the ocean.

- Ocean scientists are not sure why pom-pom anemones do not always stay attached to the sea floor like most other anemones. They may roll along the seabed when they need to look for a new place to find food.

- These anemones are not always round. They can be flat or rolled up like a tube.

Pacific viperfish

Chauliodus macouni

- This fish has a huge set of teeth. The Pacific viperfish's needle-like fangs are so big they do not even fit inside its mouth. Its two bottom teeth extend past its eyes.

- The Pacific viperfish opens its mouth wide to trap a small fish or other prey inside. Its teeth act like a cage to keep the prey from getting out. Then the viperfish swallows its prey whole.

- At night, the Pacific viperfish hunts in shallow waters where food is more plentiful. After feeding, it dives hundreds of metres back into dark waters where it is safer from predators.

- Light organs on a Pacific viperfish's belly provide a camouflage to any predators swimming below it. They cannot see the viperfish against the lighter-coloured waters.

- The viperfish uses a light at the end of the long spine on its back like a fishing lure. This light tempts the prey into coming close to the mouth of the viperfish.

- The Pacific viperfish's jaw is like a superfast hinge. In a split second, it can open its mouth as wide as its head and close its teeth around its prey just as fast.

Fact file

Lives: Pacific Ocean

Depth: 1,500 m (4,900 ft) and above

Length: 30 cm (11 ¾ in)

Diet: Small fish, shrimp and other small prey

Discovered: 1890

Balloon worm

Poeobius meseres

The balloon worm is almost completely see-through, except for its yellow gut.

Named for its oval, balloon-like shape, this worm's jelly-like body is full of fluid that helps keep it from sinking or floating up in the water.

This worm eats marine snow – small bits of droppings and dead animals that drift down from the surface. It creates a sticky mucus net to trap the food it finds.

The balloon worm drifts through the depths in an upright position, waiting for its next meal. Many other deep-sea worms crawl through the sediment on the sea floor to find food.

Flashes of blue-green light from a balloon worm's body are used to startle predators, giving the worm a chance to get away.

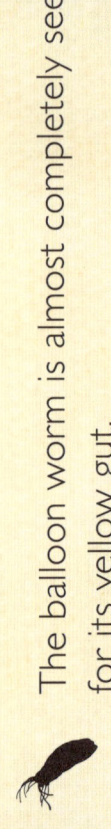

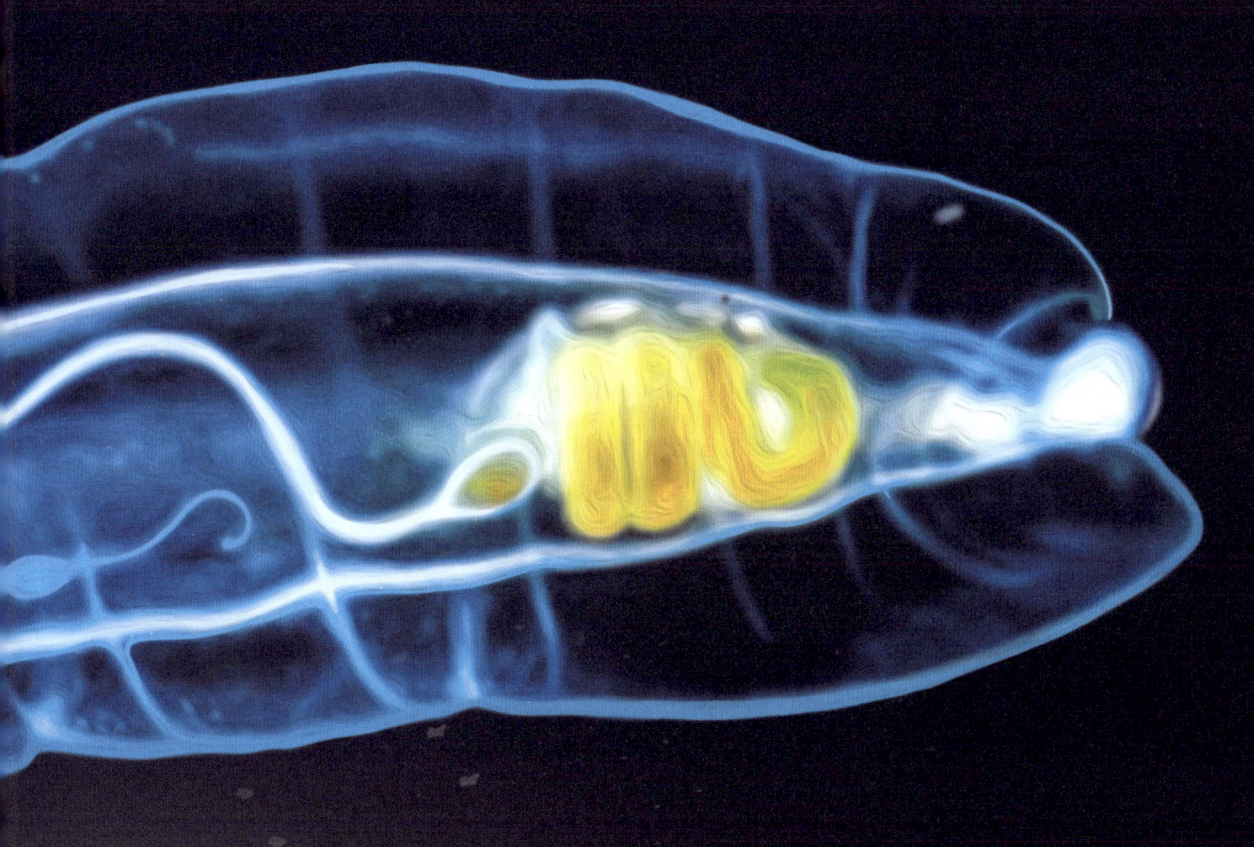

A balloon worm's tentacles are covered in small, hair-like cirri. It probably uses its tentacles to collect food and bring it to its mouth.

Fact file

Lives: Pacific Ocean
Depth: 300–2,500 m (980–8,200 ft)
Length: Up to 4 cm (1½ in)
Diet: Marine snow
Discovered: 1930

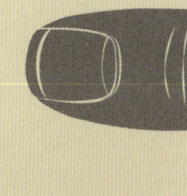

77

Piglet squid
Helicocranchia pfefferi

- What looks like a pig's snout is in fact a siphon. Siphons are the part of a squid's body that push out bursts of water to allow the creature to make powerful glides through the ocean.

- The main part of a piglet squid's body looks large and bloated because it is filled with fluid. This fluid helps it to float along in the ocean without rising towards the surface or sinking to the sea floor.

- The piglet squid usually swims while holding its short tentacles upwards. This makes it look like it has a head of spiky hair.

Fact file

Lives: Atlantic and Pacific Oceans
Depth: 1,385 m (4,540 ft) and above
Length: Approx. 10 cm (4 in)
Diet: Unknown, probably zooplankton
Discovered: 1907

- As a piglet squid gets older and bigger, it tends to move deeper into the ocean.

- The dots that decorate the piglet squid's pinkish body form small bands or stripes. A piglet squid gets darker red as it gets older.

- This squid's internal organs are visible through its almost completely see-through body. Some of these organs are clear, too.

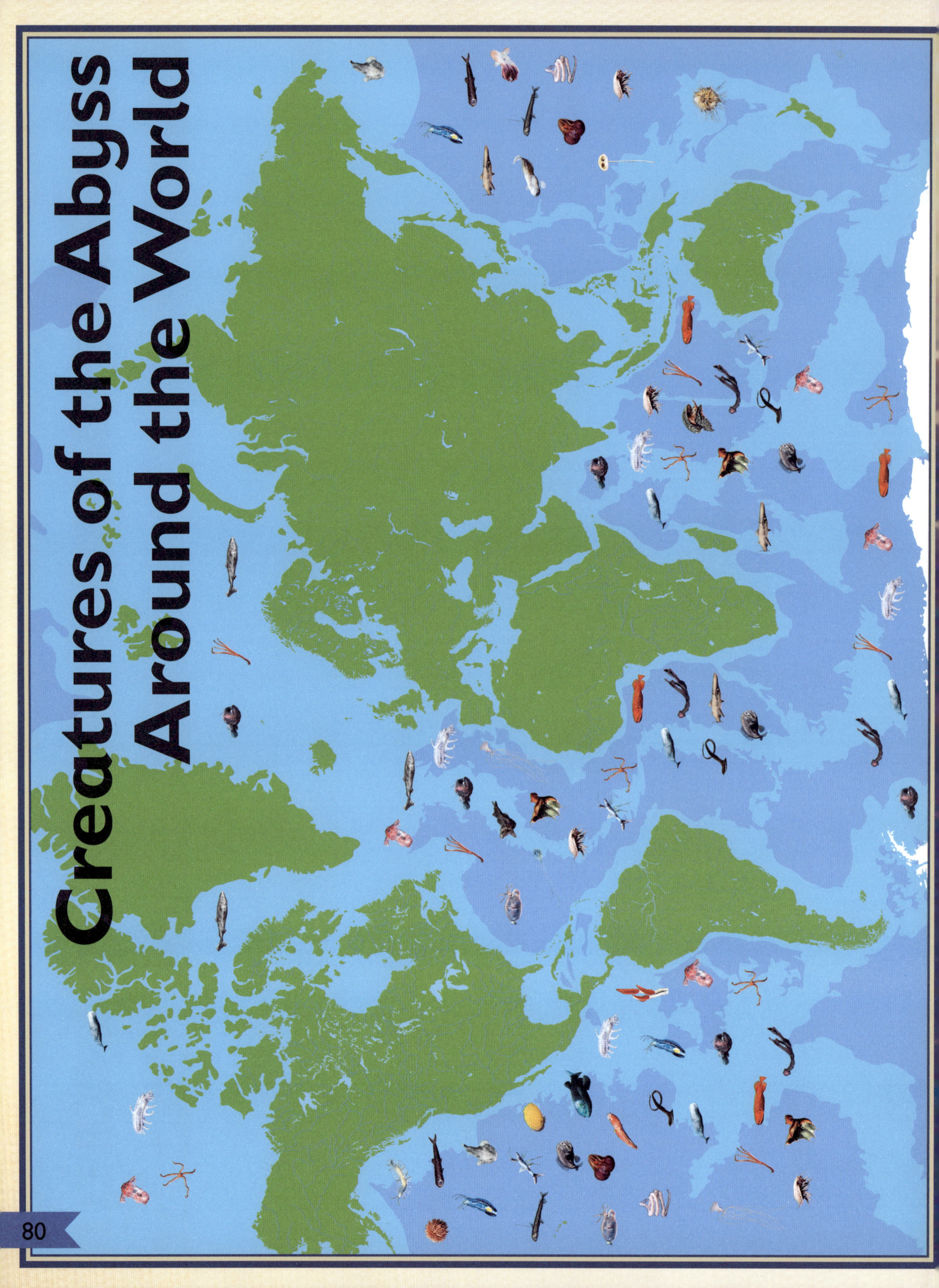